Just for Laughs

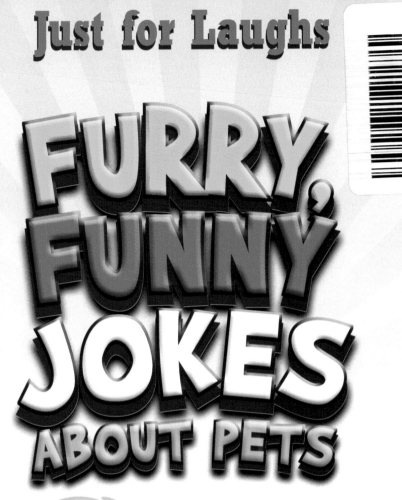

FURRY, FUNNY JOKES ABOUT PETS

Julia Garstecki

BLACK RABBIT BOOKS

Hi Jinx is published by Black Rabbit Books
P.O. Box 227, Mankato, Minnesota, 56002.
www.blackrabbitbooks.com
Copyright © 2022 Black Rabbit Books

Marysa Storm, editor; Michael Sellner, designer
and photo researcher

Library of Congress Cataloging-in-Publication Data
Names: Garstecki, Julia, author.
Title: Furry, funny jokes about pets /
by Julia Garstecki.
Description: Mankato, Minnesota :
Black Rabbit Books, [2022] | Series: Hi jinx.
Just for laughs | Includes bibliographical
references and index. | Audience: Ages: 8-12 |
Audience: Grades: 4-6 | Summary: "Through an
engaging design that brings the jokes to life
with fun facts and critical thinking questions,
Furry, Funny Jokes about Pets will have readers
laughing and learning"– Provided by publisher.
Identifiers: LCCN 2020015784 (print) |
LCCN 2020015785 (ebook) | ISBN 9781623107048
(hardcover) | ISBN 9781644665596 (paperback) |
ISBN 9781623107109 (ebook)
Subjects: LCSH: Pets–Juvenile humor. | Pets–Juvenile literature.
Classification: LCC PN6231.P42 G37 2022
(print) | LCC PN6231.P42 (ebook) | DDC 636.088/70207–dc23
LC record available at https://lccn.loc.gov/2020015784
LC ebook record available at https://lccn.loc.gov/2020015785

Image Credits

123RF: Josef Prchal, 7; iStock: cpuga, 15; davidnay, 9; StellarGraphic,
7, 23; Shutterstock: Andrey1005, 4; anfisa focusova, 4; Angeliki Vel, 19;
Christos Georghiou, 4, 12; Constantine Pankin, 18; Cory Thoman, 9;
Deniz Uzunoglu, 17; designer_an, 13; doomu, 18–19; Dualororua, 5, 8,
8–9, 9, 21; Dzianis Davydau, 9; Green angel, 3, 16; HitToon, 11; Joanne
Weston, 12; Kancut, 12; Katerina Davidenko, Cover; Katrina.Happy, 10;
KrechOksana, Cover, 6; Lal Perera, 17; LAN02, 7, 23; Lol1ta, 17; Lorelyn
Medina, Cover, 6; Memo Angeles, Cover, 1, 3, 4, 6, 7, 11, 14, 15, 16;
Muhammad Desta Laksana, 5, 17; Pasko Maksim, 18, 23, 24; Paulo
Resende, 13; picoStudio, 7, 16, 17; Pitju, 14, 21; Qualit Design, 20;
Refluo, 10, 11; Ricardo Romero, 10; Ron Dale, 5, 6, 12, 16, 20; Sararoom
Design, 19; Sergio Hayashi, 17; Stock Store, 18; Tanawat_intawong,
1; Tomacco, 10; totallypic, 18; Tueris, 14; Vector Tradition, Cover, 11;
wizdata1, 19; Yashnova Natasha, 13; Yayayoyo, 4; your, 8

CONTENTS

Chapter 1
PERFECT PETS

Some are soft, playful, and hide your socks. Others are smooth, quiet, and slither. There are many kinds of pets. And we love them all. They keep us company and help us relax. They also do hilarious, silly things. Now it's time to make them laugh in return. Learn some of these jokes, and share them with some pets. Your friends and family will appreciate them too.

Chapter 2
FURRY, FUZZY, FOUR-LEGGED FRIENDS

What is it called when a cat wins a dog show?

a cat-has-trophy

Why do cats always get their way?

They are very purr-suasive!

What's a cat's
favorite sport?

hair ball

What kind of sports car

does a cat drive?

a Furrari

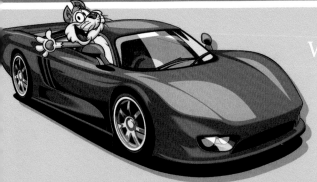

A sheepdog finished putting the sheep in a pen.
It went to the farmer and said,
"I've got all 20 sheep put away."
"But I only have 17 sheep!" cried the farmer.
"I know," said the sheepdog. "But I rounded them up."

Why are dogs
like phones?
They have collar IDs.

What did the Dalmatian
say when it finished dinner?
"That hit the spot!"

What do you call a
hamster in a top hat?

Abrahamster Lincoln

What is a ferret's favorite carnival ride?

the ferrets wheel

Did you hear about
the rich bunny?
It was a billion-hare!

What do you call a
happy guinea pig?
a grinny pig

Chapter 3
FEATHERS AND FINS

What did the fish say when it was **accused** of a crime?

"Not gill-ty!"

Why did the fish cross the ocean?

To get to the other tide.

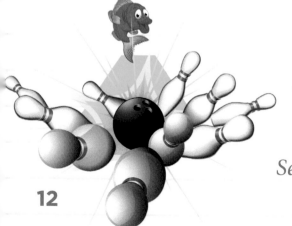

What's stranger than seeing your cat fish?

Seeing your goldfish bowl.

What happened to a school of fish
that tried to play with a piranha?

*It became a **skeleton crew**.*

What do you
call a sad bird?

a bluebird

Fun Fact
Some birds can live
more than 50 years.
That's a long time
to have a pet.

The doctor said
my bird has a cold.
Good thing it's tweetable!

What is a parrot's favorite game?
hide-and-speak

What do you get if you
cross a parrot and a shark?
A pet that talks your head off.

Chapter 4
RAD REPTILES AND AMPHIBIANS

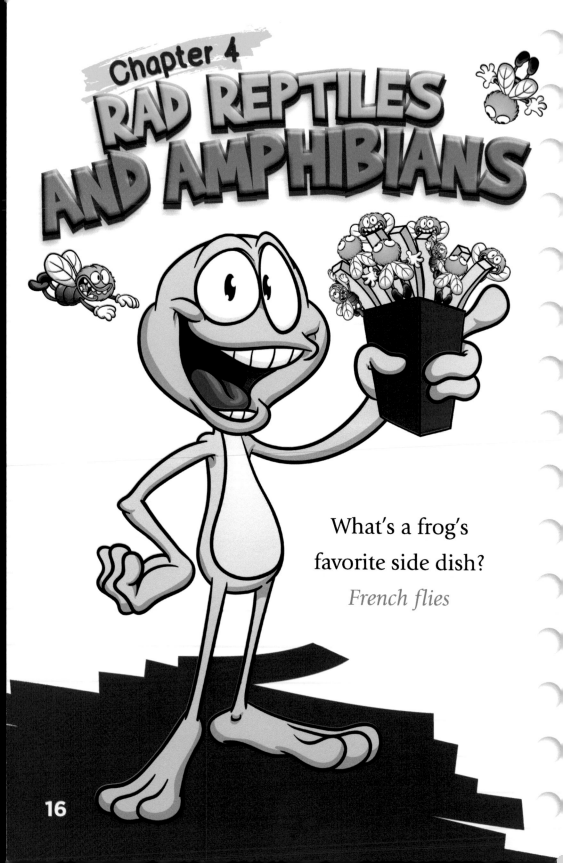

What's a frog's
favorite side dish?

French flies

What do frogs drink?

croak-a-cola

What kind of pictures
do turtles take?

shellfies

What did the frog think
of the bedtime story?

*It thought the
story was ribbiting.*

17

Fun Fact

There are more than 3,000 different snake species. Not all of them make good pets.

How do you

measure your snake?

In inches. They don't have feet.

What happens when
you put your snake
back in its **terrarium**?

It throws a hissy fit!

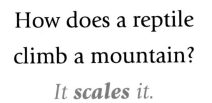

How does a reptile
climb a mountain?

*It **scales** it.*

19

Chapter 5
Get in on the Hi Jinx

If you enjoy pet jokes, you might want a job working with animals someday. There are many options. One job is pet groomer. Pet groomers wash and style pet hair and fur. They also do nails. Some even shave shapes into fur or **dye** it different colors. For the time being, you can get creative with these jokes.

Take It One Step More

1. Other than pet groomer, what other jobs deal with animals? Would you like any of them?

2. Pick a joke from the book that made you laugh. Write a similar joke about your dream pet.

3. What jokes weren't funny to you? Can you think of a way to make them funnier?

GLOSSARY

accuse (uh-KYOOZ)—to blame for something wrong or illegal

dye (DAHY)—to change the color of something using a substance

scale (SKAYL)—to climb; it is also one of the small stiff plates that cover much of the body of some animals.

shed (SHED)—to lose or cast aside a natural covering or part

skeleton crew (SKEL-i-tn KROO)—just enough workers to keep a service or office operating

species (SPEE-seez)—a class of individuals that have common characteristics and share a common name

terrarium (tuh-RAIR-ee-uhm)—a glass or plastic box that is used for growing plants or keeping small animals indoors

BOOKS

Dahl, Michael, and Mark Ziegler. *Michael Dahl's Big Book of Jokes.* Michael Dahl Presents. North Mankato, MN: Stone Arch Books, 2020.

Garstecki, Julia. *Silly, Smelly Animal Jokes.* Just for Laughs. Mankato, MN: Black Rabbit Books, 2018.

Winn, Whee. *Lots of Animal Jokes for Kids.* Grand Rapids, MI: Zonderkidz, 2020.

WEBSITES

11 Funny Animal Jokes for Kids (and Kids at Heart) **nationalzoo.si.edu/animals/news/11-funny-animal-jokes-for-kids-and-kids-heart**

Animal Jokes: Funology Jokes and Riddles **www.funology.com/animal-jokes/**

Jokes for Kids: Big List of Animal Jokes **www.ducksters.com/jokes/animals.php**